How to Stop Overthinking

8 Proven, Practical Techniques to End Anxiety, Stop Negative Thinking, Overcome Worrying and Live a Healthier, Happier Life.

(Change Your Life Series, Book 1)

By

Charles P. Carlton

Copyright © 2019 – Charles P. Carlton

All rights reserved

No part of this publication may be reproduced, distributed, or transmitted in any form or by any means, including photocopying, recording, or other electronic or mechanical methods, without the prior written permission of the publisher, except in the case of brief quotations embodied in reviews and certain other non-commercial uses permitted by copyright law.

Disclaimer

This publication is designed to provide competent and reliable information regarding the subject matter covered. However, the views expressed in this publication are those of the author alone, and should not be taken as expert instruction or professional advice. The reader is responsible for his or her own actions.

The author hereby disclaims any responsibility or liability whatsoever that is incurred from the use or application of the contents of this publication by the purchaser or reader.

Table of Contents

Books By The Same Authors 7

Free Gift 8

About The Author 9

Introduction 10

Section I – An Introduction to Overthinking and Its Impact on Your Life 14

Chapter 1 15

Let's Get Started 15

    How Our Brain Works When We Overthink? 15

    What Overthinking Is and Isn't? 18

    Causes of Overthinking 20

    Signs You Are Being Controlled by Overthinking 21

    Effects of Overthinking on You 23

    Case Study 26

    Practice Test 26

Chapter 2 28

Anxiety, Negative Thought and Worry 28

    What Triggers These Feelings? 29

    Write Them Down in a Journal 32

    Why You Should Write Them Down 34

    Case Study 35

    Practice Test 36

Section II – Techniques to Stop Overthinking 39

Chapter 3 40

Reflect on the Bright Side of Life Everyday 40

    You Can't Change the Past or Predict the Future: Live in the Present 40

    Change the Way You Think: Gratitude Vs. Regret 43

    Act with Confidence: Stop Asking "What If"? 46

    Do Away with Negativity and Embrace Positivity 47

    Case Study 48

    Practice Test 49

Chapter 4 53

Create a To-Do List 53

How Your Life would be Without a To-Do List 54

How a To-Do List Helps with Overthinking 55

Maintain a To-Do List & Stick to it 57

Case Study 64

Practice Test 65

Chapter 5 67

Live a Minimalist Lifestyle 67

What is Minimalism? 67

Benefits of a Minimalist Lifestyle? 68

How to Apply Minimalism in Your Everyday Life 69

Case Study 77

Practice Test 78

Chapter 6 79

Get Rid of the Past and Bad Relationships 79

Get Unstuck from Your Ugly Memories 79

How You Can Identify a Bad Relationship 81

Let Go of Certain People 86

Tips to Shake Off Bad Relationships from Your Life 88

- Case Study 91
- Practice Test 93

Chapter 7 94
Pursue Your Goals 94
- Discover Your Vocation 95
- What Motivates You? – Your Passions 100
- Note Down Your Life Goals 102
- Connect Goals to Passions and Prioritize Them 104
- Set S.M.A.R.T. Goals 106
- How to Set S.M.A.R.T. Goals that WORKS! 107
- Case Study 110
- Practice Test 111

Chapter 8 114
Practice Mindfulness 114
- What is Mindfulness? 114
- Why You Need to Practice Mindfulness 115
- Effective Techniques for Practicing Mindfulness 117
- Case Study 137

Practice Test 137

Chapter 9 139

Be Happy 139

    Live Your Best Life: There Is Only One to Live 140

    Steps You Can Take to Be Happy 141

    Case Study 144

    Practice Test 145

Chapter 10 148

Reach Out to Someone 148

    Don't be Afraid to Ask for Help 149

    Talk to a Physician If Everything Else Fails 152

    Case Study 153

    Practice Test 153

Conclusion 155

Books By The Same Authors

Cognitive Behavioral Therapy Made Simple (Change Your Life Series, Book 2)

Master Your Emotions (2 Books in 1)

Stop Overthinking and Vagus Nerve Stimulation (2 Books in 1)

Free Gift

In expression of my gratitude for purchasing my book, I am offering you a free copy of my *Bulletproof Self-Esteem* companion guide, proven to boost your self-confidence in **ONE WEEK**.

To have instant access to this gift, type this link http://bit.ly/346qi8P into your web browser, or you can send an email to charlescarltonpublishing@gmail.com, and I would get your copy across to you.

About The Author

Charles P. Carlton, a former consultant with a top big 4 global consulting firm, Ernst & Young and a Fortune 100 best companies to work for is a self-help professional, devoted to showing you the tricks on how to hack your life to get the most out of it by getting things done.

His quest for self-discovery led him to retire from the corporate world to fulfill his life-long goals of being a self-help coach and writer.

He specializes in using a cut-through science-based and personal experience approach in connecting with his audience in areas of emotional intelligence, self-esteem, and self-confidence, self-discovery, communication, personal development, and productivity. This has helped him build successful relationships and connections with his audience.

When not writing, Charles loves reading and exploring the beauty of nature from where most times he gets many thought-provoking inspirations.

Introduction

"You only have control over three things in your life – the thoughts you think, the images you visualize, and the actions your take."

— Jack Canfield

This book contains important information, guidelines, and tips on how to prevent and stop you from overthinking and keep your feelings of anxiety, negative thoughts, and worries at bay.

When the stress and demands of modern life get out of hand, people tend to lose their grip over their thoughts and emotions. Many find it hard to rein in their insecurities and doubts about the situation they are currently in. As a result, they fall victim to the analysis paralysis.

At that point, the person feels stuck in a miserable loop of anxious feelings, negative thoughts, and worries. Overcoming this can be quite a difficult feat to achieve—but it is not impossible.

You are more than your thoughts and emotions. You can break free from your past, be more content with living in the moment and be more receptive to the future. You can also do away with certain feelings or things around your home, workplace and relationships that trigger the anxieties, negative thoughts and worries that besiege you. All of these are possible if you make a conscious decision today to take control of your life and change your course for the better.

To accomplish this feat, you need to make significant changes not only in the way you think but also the way you handle your relationships with yourself and the people around you.

This book shall serve as a guide for you to understand better what overthinking is and what it does to different aspects of your life. Reading through the first section of this book shall also help you recognize and identify the sources of your feelings of anxiety, negative thoughts, and worries.

From this point on, you are encouraged to keep a personal journal by your side as you continue reading in order to document your responses to the practice tests in the succeeding chapters of this book. This is critical because you need to see for yourself how the proposed techniques to stop overthinking can be applied to your personal issues.

As attested by multiple studies conducted over the years by mental health experts, the suggested techniques in the second section of this book can help you reduce—if not totally eliminate—the detrimental effects of overthinking and anxiety in various areas of your life.

These techniques can help you:

- improve how you regard your past, present, and future;
- better manage your daily tasks to avoid analysis paralysis;
- eliminate the non-essential things and toxic people in your life;
- improve your chances of achieving your personal goals and finding happiness; and
- get more comfortable about seeking help and of those who care for you, and from those who are qualified to give you the mental health care that you need.

Do not suffer in silence when you have at your fingertips the possible ways out of your current situation. As an author and public speaker, Ken Poirot once emphasized in his book "Mentor Me," "Right now is the best time to create your tomorrow."

Read each chapter carefully, and reflect on how you can apply the points covered to stop overthinking, anxiety, negative thinking, and worrying.

In the words of Zig Ziglar, "People often say that motivation doesn't last. Well, neither does bathing – that's why we recommend it daily."

Hence to stop overthinking using any of the techniques laid out in this book, you have to apply it continuously.

Thanks for downloading this book. I hope you enjoy it!

Section I – An Introduction to Overthinking and Its Impact on Your Life

Chapter 1

Let's Get Started

"The more you overthink, the less you will understand."

— Habeeb Akande

The path towards a happy and fulfilling life begins with unloading your mind of its unnecessary burdens. Overthinking is considered by many as a natural human behavior. However, this does not mean that you should only accept this without even attempting to counteract its negative effects on the quality of your life.

Before delving deeper into how you can stop yourself from overthinking, you must learn how to recognize the signs that you are engaging in overthinking.

How Our Brain Works When We Overthink?

Overthinking happens when the brain becomes too caught up with certain thoughts, thus causing the person to fail in acting upon the said thoughts. It is essentially a mental state wherein the brain is trapped in a cycle of repeated analysis over the same topic or issue.

As a result, energy is expended unnecessarily, while signs of mental strain begin manifesting in the individual's day-to-day activities and even in one's interactions with other people.

To better demonstrate how the brain works when it is engaged in overthinking, go through the following list of scenarios—some of which may even sound familiar to you:

- You cannot stop thinking about a personal problem or an event that has already transpired. Rather than focus on how to solve your current predicament, you cannot seem to pull yourself away from these thoughts. No matter what you do, your thoughts keep coming back to the problem or the event itself—not what you can do to get yourself out of this situation.

- Something terrible has happened to you. As a result, you cannot seem to stop asking yourself why that has happened to you. You also find yourself ruminating about what would have happened instead if only you had done things a little differently.

- Your mind jumps into the worst conclusions, even without any solid or sound basis at all. It has been occurring to your regularly, so that, by now, the negative thoughts appear to be following some sort of pattern in your head.

- You find yourself obsessing about the tiny details in your day-to-day experiences, especially when it involves interacting with those around you.

- You even come up with dialogues in your head, recreating mentally certain life events where you think you could have done better.

- You assign meaning to every word, thought, and action that sometimes goes beyond what is reasonable and realistic. People also say that you read into things, only to realize later on that they are not worth your time and effort.

If you recognize yourself in any of these scenarios, and if you think that such scenarios happen to you frequently, then you might be falling into the habit of overthinking.

As shown in the examples above, addressing this issue is of the utmost importance. Overthinking is keeping you from moving forward and experiencing new things in life. It is like having your hand-tied with a rope that is attached to a pole. You can only go around in circles around the same thing, over and over again.

What Overthinking Is and Isn't?

Right off the bat, it should be made clear that overthinking is not a form of mental illness. It is, however, a common symptom that can be observed among different types of anxiety disorders.

For example, Ben has been diagnosed with panic disorder. He is prone to overthink about when the next panic attack might happen. If he thinks something might trigger an attack, he cannot help himself but obsess over this possibility. As such, his tendency to overthink these triggers only serves to increase the risk of panic attacks.

You do not have to be suffering from an anxiety disorder to engage in overthinking. This is an all-too-common human experience that happens almost naturally to everyone.

You may feel concerned over what you have said to your friend the last time you talked over the phone. Perhaps, you are worried about an upcoming test or job interview. You might feel a little too conscious about how others perceive you at work. These are just some examples of common scenarios where overthinking is at play.

It should also be noted that there is a distinction between the two forms of overthinking:

- brooding over the past

    Dwelling about the mistakes you have done, and the opportunities you have missed out on can be detrimental to your current happiness and mental state.

- worrying about the future

    The uncertainty of what will happen next can trap a person into a never-ending cycle of "what-ifs" and "should-I's".

Overthinking is also different from introspection. The latter involves gaining personal insights and fresh personal perspectives about a certain matter. You introspect with a clear purpose in mind.

Overthinking, on the other hand, involves negative feelings about things that are usually outside of your control. As such, you will not feel like you have progressed at all after engaging in overthinking.

Causes of Overthinking

There is no single origin or trigger for one to engage in overthinking. It can be born out of genuine worry for one's welfare and those of others. Some overthink as a result of how they have been conditioned to think by their parents, their teachers, and their peers.

Extreme forms of overthinking are believed to be rooted in certain mental and psychological issues that a person is suffering from. These include but are not limited to:

- post-traumatic stress disorder (PTSD);
- panic disorder;
- social anxiety disorder;
- substance-induced anxiety disorder;
- separation anxiety disorder;
- different types of phobias, particularly agoraphobia; and
- physical, mental, and/or emotional trauma.

Linking mental health issues with overthinking, however, is not as straightforward as it may seem. Some experts suggest that overthinking contributes to the decline of one's mental health. However, others are reporting that existing mental health problems can trigger a person to engage in overthinking.

Giving a definitive answer on the actual cause of overthinking, therefore, can get you stuck in a loop. The actual case may also vary from one individual to another.

Rather than ruminate over the exact origin of overthinking, you should focus instead on learning how to assess yourself for signs of overthinking. Through this, you will be able to check if your tendency to overthink is getting out of hand already.

Signs You Are Being Controlled by Overthinking

Much like any human behavior, the effects of overthinking can be described as a dichotomy.

On one end, overthinking may be considered helpful since it allows a person to learn from past experiences and prevent the recurrence of certain mistakes in the future. When used in this way, overthinking can be beneficial in terms of problem solving and decision-making.

The problem begins when these thoughts become excessive, thus creating anxiety, stress, and a sense of fear and dread within the person. At this point, overthinking has gone beyond simply thinking too much about a person or a thing—overthinking has become an obsession that disrupts an individual's capacity to function and interact with other people.

If you are experiencing at least one of the following situations, then it's evident that you are being controlled by overthinking:

- Continually measuring your worth, success, and happiness against the people around you;

- Focusing on the worst possible outcomes whenever you or someone you care for is involved in something risky or dangerous;

- Having trouble in keeping up with and contributing to conversations because you go over your potential responses for too long that either you miss the appropriate timing for your responses, or the conversation itself has already ended;

- Worrying about future activities and task that you must accomplish so much that you feel overwhelmed at just the thought of having to do any of them;

- Repeatedly thinking about personal mistakes and failures from the past, thus preventing you from moving on with your life;

- Repeatedly reliving past trauma, loss, or abusive situation that robs you of your chance to cope with it;

- Failing to calm down your racing thoughts and overwhelming but vague emotions that seemingly manifest out of nowhere.

Please note that the signs of overthinking, as highlighted above, are not exhaustive. However, if you find yourself continuously thinking about certain aspects of your life, or you find yourself in an endless cycle of non-productive thoughts, then that in itself is a sign that you are embroiled in overthinking.

Effects of Overthinking on You

No matter how similar the circumstances are between two people, their respective manner of overthinking would not be the same. As such, the effects of overthinking would be felt differently by each individual.

It has been observed by psychologists, however, that those who cannot control their tendency to overthink suffer from a decreased quality of life. To give you a background on the possible effects of overthinking in your life, here are some common examples of difficulties faced by those who have been identified as chronic over-thinkers:

- Making new friends or keeping the ones they already have can be tough due to their struggles in effectively communicating their thoughts and feelings.

- They find it hard to go out and have fun doing their hobbies because they have already spent their time and energy ruminating about certain matters inside their heads.

- Setting up appointments, or even simply going to the store can be an arduous task for them.

- Taking and exercising full control of their thoughts and emotions seem impossible because their mind is already strained and overworked.

Looking through these points, you can surmise that overthinking can ruin your relationships, isolate you from the rest of the world, and it can increase your risk of developing other serious mental issues, such as depression and anxiety disorder.

The bottom line is that overthinking has wide-reaching effects in almost everything you do and want to do in life. It does not only impose limits on you but also to those who wish to express their support to you. This means that overthinking can create serious problems not only in your personal abilities but also the kind of relationships that you will have.

Currently, there is no single form of treatment that you can adopt to completely relieve yourself of overthinking and its negative effects on you. Perhaps, one day, the mental health community would be able to come up with the ultimate solution for this.

However, this should not stop you from seeking out methods that can help you control your thoughts and eliminate your tendency to overthink. This book shall help you understand and apply the strategies that would work best for you, given the peculiarity of your situation.

Case Study

Amy is a middle-school teacher who frequently found herself worried about what people thought of her as a person, and how people see her worth as a teacher. Whenever she interacted with a parent or a co-teacher, she would usually pause for a second or two to figure out if her words were appropriate or offensive.

At times, Amy would be filled with dread as question upon question began flooding her head. She would attempt to answer all of them, but doing so did not alleviate the stress and discomfort that she felt.

When her overthinking began affecting the quality of her work, Amy decided that it is time to find a way out of the miserable recurring situation. She did not, however, want to settle for a short-term solution.

What Amy wanted was to find a way to stop overthinking for good. She had admitted to herself that something was wrong and that serious steps must be taken as soon as possible. This acknowledgment by itself was a huge step towards her goal.

Practice Test

If you have a similar goal with Amy, you need to take a moment and recognize the effects of overthinking in your life. This will be part of your motivation to pursue your goal to overcome overthinking.

In your personal journal, describe specific incidents in the following key areas of your life where your incessant thoughts have taken over your good sense.

- a. Family
- b. Friendship ✓
- c. Romantic Relationship
- d. Work
- e. Health and Fitness

Then, answer the following questions right after your responses for each area:

- What do you think triggered you to engage in overthinking?
- How did it make you feel at the time?
- How do you feel about that incident now?

Chapter 2

Anxiety, Negative Thought and Worry

"Overthinking can lead to worrying, which leads to anxiety. Anxiety can, at times, be crippling, leave people frozen and unable to act. Overthinking can also lead to depression. Either of these can leave you unable to focus, feeling hopeless, and irritable."

— Brien Blatt

Anxiety is wherein an individual suffers from uncontrollable negative thoughts and excessive feelings of worry. Some people also experience physical symptoms of anxiety, such as chest pains and trembling.

There is no single cause that triggers anxiety, negative thought, or worry. Experts suggest that these feelings originate from the combination of various factors, including genetics and one's external environment.

What is clear at this point is that certain emotions, experiences, and instances can bring out or even worsen the symptoms of anxiety. These factors are referred to as triggers.

What Triggers These Feelings?

Triggers of anxiety, negative thought, and worry vary from one person to another. However, these triggers can be categorized into their probable sources, such as:

- Romantic Relationships

    Relationships are a landmine of potential triggers for anxiety, negative thought, and worry. Even when a couple is just at the start of their relationship, the novelty of being together with another person can put a strain on one's mental and emotional health.

    Having arguments or disagreements with one's partner can be particularly stressful at any point in the relationship. If the couple are not effective communicators, the lack of conflict resolution between them may trigger feelings.

- Family Matters

    You cannot choose your family, so even when they make you feel upset or unhappy, it is nearly impossible to cut them off from your life completely. As a result, spending time with them may cause you to feel elevated anxiety levels and increased negative thoughts.

Becoming a parent is typically one of the biggest life milestones that a person can have. Even though it is most exciting, the new responsibilities that this entails can be a trigger for many people.

They may experience doubts about whether or not they will make good parents. Some are also worried about the strain that this will cause to their career, social life, and personal finances.

- Friendships

    Much like your romantic relationships, your friendships may trigger your anxiety, especially when you disagree with your friends. You may also begin harboring negative thoughts about them if you fail to communicate with them effectively. Worrying about the future of your friendship with them would then be a common thing, especially when you begin questioning yourself if you should stay friends with them.

- Jobs and Career

Your current job and career may cause you to feel these things, especially when you do not enjoy what you are doing. Forcing yourself to work for something that is not your true calling can lead you further into a boring, depressing, and unfulfilled life.

- Money

    Financial worries, such as paying off a debt or having to save up money, are commonly felt by people who suffer from these feelings. Unexpected bills and sudden financial instability have also been identified as strong triggers for many individuals.

- Loss

    Loss is often associated with intense feelings of sadness, regret, and fear. An individual who has recently experienced the loss of a loved one may feel anxious about what their life would be from then on. They may also have negative thoughts about the circumstances that have led to the said loss. Some may even feel particularly worried that they will never recover from their grief and that they will never feel normal again.

- Trauma

    Personal traumas, whether they are physical, verbal, or sexual, are particularly harrowing experiences for anyone. They tend to have long-lasting effects, especially when the person cannot help but relieve that specific moment in his/her head over and over again.

- Health Issues

    Receiving an unexpected and/or upsetting diagnosis, especially when it pertains to serious chronic illnesses, can trigger one's anxiety, negative thought, and worry.

    Because it is deeply personal, the after-effects of receiving such news are usually intensely felt by the individual.

Many people report having more than one trigger for their anxiety, negative thoughts, and worries. Some experience anxiety attacks with no apparent trigger.

Because of this, you must assess yourself and find out what may trigger these feelings within you. By doing so, you will be able to manage them better later on.

Write Them Down in a Journal

An effective strategy to accurately identify your triggers is to start a journal that is dedicated to recording your experiences and feelings related to anxiety, negative thought, and worry.

You do not have to be a skilled writer to keep a journal. As long as you can communicate your thoughts and feelings in written form, then journaling can be an effective personal management tool for you.

Do not worry about grammar rules or spelling. You do not also have to limit yourself to what is socially acceptable or politically correct. This journal is your personal safe space, where you can reveal your true self.

To guide you through this process, here are some valuable tips that you may apply:

- Look for a place where you can write without being distracted or interrupted.

- Try to write in your journal at least once a day.

- When writing about personal trauma, try focusing on your feelings about the incident rather than the details of the said trauma.

- Give yourself time to reflect upon what you have written down.

- Keep your journal away from prying eyes by storing it somewhere secure.

Why You Should Write Them Down

By writing down your experiences and feelings in a journal, you will be able to:

- give yourself more time to process them later on;
- become more objective when it comes to evaluating and dealing with personal matters;
- increase your tolerance for your anxiety triggers and the various stresses of your daily life;
- transform your negative energy into something more open and creative; and
- gain an insight into how you can move forward from these experiences and feelings.

Feeling anxious, having a negative thought, and being worried are natural parts of being human—as long as they happen to you occasionally. However, experiencing these on a chronic level is a sign that there are deeper issues at play here.

If these feelings are starting to affect the quality of your day-to-day life, then you must learn how to accept the fact that you need help, and that you need to act upon this matter soon.

Case Study

Having decided to work on stopping her tendency to overthink, Amy believed that the best way to start this was to document her journey throughout the entire process. In this way, she would be able to look back at her notes and reflect upon the probable strategies she could take.

Since Amy had already identified and recognized the problem, what she wanted to do at this point was to determine the variables that caused her to overthink. She broke her list down into three: anxiety, negative thinking, and worries. Under each, she added the following sub-categories: family, friends, romantic relationship, work, money, and health.

Over two weeks, Amy wrote down in the journal her personal observations about what triggers her overthinking. She took her time to assign each to their corresponding categories.

When she was done, she looked over her list and found out that most of her triggers were work-related. Of these triggers, three recurring themes had emerged. Her confidence as a teacher could be easily shaken by a comment from a colleague. She felt apprehensive whenever parents would approach her to inquire about the behavior of their children within the classroom. An upcoming performance appraisal on her was also worrying her for some time now.

Following Pareto's 80/20 rule—wherein 80% of her problems would be resolved by working on 20% of her list—Amy was now ready to try out potential solutions to her problem with overthinking.

Practice Test

Refer back to the list you have created during the practice test for the previous chapter. Just like what Amy did, identify the triggers for your anxiety, negative thoughts, and worries that caused you to overthink excessively.

Follow this table format in recording your responses:

Feelings of Anxiety	Negative Thoughts	Worries

Romantic Relationship			
Family Matters			
Friendship			
Job & Career			
Money			
Loss			
Trauma			
Health			

Next, try to highlight the common themes in your responses. To get the most out of your efforts, it is best to stick to resolving a few issues that can potentially cause a bigger impact on the achievement of your goal.

Recurring Theme #1: _____

Recurring Theme #2: _____

Recurring Theme #3: _____

Section II – Techniques to Stop Overthinking

Chapter 3

Reflect on the Bright Side of Life Everyday

"Once you replace negative thoughts with positive ones, you'll start having positive results."

—Willie Nelson

You Can't Change the Past or Predict the Future: Live in the Present

Living in the present can be a difficult feat to achieve for many. Whether it is through their upbringing or as a result of various environmental factors, most people have been conditioned to dwell about the past and to worry about the future. Even today's technology contributes to one's inability to focus on the present.

Take, for example, the notifications you receive from your phone. You may be fully engrossed in whatever you are doing at the moment. Still, when you hear your phone go off, the mind tends to automatically switch to either a past experience or a future event related to the notification you have received.

Other factors that can keep you from staying in the present include:

- the natural tendency of the mind to edit out the positive aspects of your previous experiences, thus making the past seem more negative than it was; and

- the uncertainty of the current situation you are in, which then generates feelings of anxiety, negative thoughts, and worry.

Many people find it difficult to overcome these elements and start living in the present. Some do not even know what it means to be in the present. They cannot imagine how it feels like to be free from their ruminations about the past, and their apprehensions about the future. Most of the time, they simply do not have enough personal will to focus on what is currently happening to them.

Fortunately, there are various ways to get over the challenges of being in the here and now. Through the right mindset and a positive attitude, you can start living in the present and make better life choices.

When you live in acceptance of what has already happened, and what will come to pass, then you will begin seeing things for what they truly are. You will be able to forgive yourself and others for the mistakes that have been made in the past. You will also be able to free yourself from feelings of anxiety and worry about the things that may come your way.

Let me share my personal experience on this subject!

So, it just happens that I had made at some point in my life, quite too many financial mistakes and bad financial investments that did cost me some huge chunk of my savings for the supposed pleasant life I looked forward to living. Not once, not twice, not even thrice. Under these circumstances, I should have typically read the signs on the wall, right? and know what investment is good and bad, but duh! *(laughs),* I kept sinking in much money in more investments, but this time around, in a bid to recover my previous financial losses. However, I ended up losing more and more. At a point, I lost it and went into bouts of anxiety, negative thoughts, and worries about the mess I created in my finances and how I should have known better after the initial three losses incurred. I would overthink what would become of my financial status, especially at the point of my life where I was somewhat out of a job. I was scared, unhappy, and angry every other day I lived. This feeling went on for as long as I could remember, and then, on one Tuesday morning, I laid woken right on my bed and looked up, gazing into the ceiling before me, and I asked myself, a life-changing question.

"How has my overthinking of the past financial mistakes, what I could have done differently, and what the life I hoped to live in the future has helped me achieve?".

I decided that I was going to leave the past mistakes where it belongs, "the past"— I was going to focus on living in the present by making the most out of it— and that I wasn't going to beat myself up about what the future holds. Consciously deciding on this gave me a great sense of relief and peace.

No matter how much we try, we can't change the past simply because it is out of our control, and no matter how we wish we could predict the future, we simply can't because the universe operates on its terms and conditions. So then, the obvious choice you can make, one which you have control of is to live in the moment and enjoy what each day brings. It sure helps.

Change the Way You Think: Gratitude Vs. Regret
Everyone has felt regret at different points in life. You may have gotten over them by now, but you have

surely experienced how heavy regrets can be.

Regret can be something you have done—whether deliberately or unintentionally—that have hurt yourself or somebody else. You may also feel regret after making a snap decision that resulted in something less favorable than it should have been had you only taken your time.

Having regrets is a normal human experience. Obsessing over them, however, is not healthy nor productive, and would most likely result to overthinking which in turn would produce bouts of anxiety, negative thoughts and worry. There is no way to go back in time and change the circumstances that have led to those regrets. The only way to go is forward.

To overcome a regretful mindset, you must learn how to adapt and apply gratitude in your life. Rather than ruminating about what has happened and what could have been, you should switch your attention to the good things that are happening in your life.

Changing the way you think is not something you can do half-heartedly. You must learn how to practice gratitude whichever way you can. You can do it by literally keeping track of the fortunate instances you have experienced in life. Others find the habit of writing down positive things to help keep them grateful, especially during tough times.

You can even take this further by being thankful for the lessons you have gained from your past, no matter how painful or hard they are. Be thankful that you have managed to live through them, and you have then been given the opportunity to learn from your past mistakes. You are now a step closer to enlightenment and becoming a better version of you.

Once you have chosen to adopt a grateful mindset fully, then you will be able to:

- feel contentment about the blessings in your life;
- gain an optimistic point of view;
- better appreciate the people around you;
- find ways to help those in need; and
- have a higher level of self-awareness.

Take note that successfully overcoming your regrets does not happen overnight. You must be patient with yourself, and continually practice applying gratitude in all aspects of your life. The more you practice it, the easier it becomes to access a grateful mindset, even during trying times.

Act with Confidence: Stop Asking "What If"?

Torturing yourself with the question "what if" gives you nothing but unnecessary feelings of anxiety, negative thoughts, and worry. There is no way to know for sure what will exactly happen by choosing to act in a certain way. It is a waste of time and energy to think about the uncontrollable aspects of the future.

More often than not, obsessing over the possible outcomes of your actions will only make you feel upset. Having no definite answer since there is an endless number of possibilities can be particularly unsettling.

To stop asking yourself this question, you must:

- focus on the here and now of the situation;
- identify the things that are within your control; and
- think of each situation as an opportunity to learn.

If you do end up acting upon the wrong decision, the only healthy thing to do is to learn from it and move on. Do not let your mistake define your present and what your future would become.

Reallocate the time and energy you would have used in overthinking about the what-ifs of the situation into something more productive. Use that as a motivation to make better decisions the next time you are facing a similar circumstance. Remember, you can take more control over your thoughts and actions if you would simply believe you can do so.

Do Away with Negativity and Embrace Positivity

There are days when nothing seems to go your way. The moment you wake up, you just know everything that can go wrong will go wrong.

Since you are already expecting it, any disappointment that comes your way further strengthens the negative vibes that you are feeling. When this happens over and over again, those vibes solidify into a perennial negative mindset.

If this scenario sounds familiar to you, then know that you have the option to turn things around for the better. You are in control, and you can choose how you are going to approach important matters in your life.

From here, you can start nurturing a positive mindset that is centered around your personal growth and development. You can reframe your outlook in life, thus giving you hope and motivation to overcome the challenges that may come your way.

It should be noted that you should actively work on embracing positivity. Once you have acknowledged that you have the right to be happy and that you are ultimately responsible for your happiness, you may then proceed to apply this positive mindset in your day to day life, and the achievement of your goals.

Case Study

While searching for effective strategies to combat the negative effects of overthinking and anxiety, Amy stumbled upon the various research works conducted on the field of positive psychology. There, she learned that she had to let go of what had happened to her in the past to give space to a more positive present and future. She had also realized that her regrets about missed opportunities back in her days at the university were bogging her down.

While writing down these reflections in her journal, Amy decided to apply some of the techniques she had read about. First, she made a list of the blessings and things she feels grateful for in her life. Then, she copied each on a separate sticky note.

Since the most of her triggers were work-related, she posted the said sticky notes on a board beside her work desk. In that way, she could easily see them whenever she needed a boost.

Over a week, she recorded in her journal how she felt after a few minutes of staying at her work desk. She had noted small but steady increments in her mood day by day. There was one positive fluctuation, however, when she took the time to read through some of the posted notes.

Given her observations, Amy resolved to make a habit of counting her blessings and remind herself of what she was thankful for.

Practice Test

Create your gratitude list based on the people, things, and life events that you feel thankful for in different aspects of your life. Follow this suggested format so that you can use this list to answer the following questions.

- Romantic Relationship

    a. _____

    b. _____

    c. _____

d. _____

e. _____

- Family

    a. _____

    b. _____

    c. _____

    d. _____

    e. _____

- Friendship

    a. _____

    b. _____

    c. _____

    d. _____

    e. _____

- Job & Career

    a. _____

    b. _____

       c. _____

       d. _____

       e. _____

- Money

       a. _____

       b. _____

       c. _____

       d. _____

       e. _____

- Health

       a. _____

       b. _____

       c. _____

       d. _____

       e. _____

- Others

       a. _____

b. _____

c. _____

d. _____

e. _____

Based on your responses, answer the following questions:

- How do you feel after writing down this list?

- Which category/categories contains the most number of listed items? Describe how you feel about that particular aspect of your life.

- Which category/categories contains the least number of listed items? Describe how you feel about that particular aspect of your life.

- Do you possess a more positive or more negative outlook in life? Why do you think so?

Chapter 4

Create a To-Do List

"Each day, I will accomplish one thing on my to-do list."

— Lailah Gifty Akita

A to-do list is one of the most basic, yet easily overlooked, task management tool at anyone's disposal. Essentially, a to-do list contains information about what you should be doing, how it should be done, and when it must be done.

The principle behind a to-do list is quite simple. It has also been around for so long. However, no matter how simple it is, the problem with a to-do list is that people tend to forget about them eventually.

Some find it too simple that they think it is not effective in serving its purpose. Others recognize the importance and merits of a to-do list, but they lack the discipline in maintaining one in the long run.

To better illustrate to you why you should create and keep a to-do list, the next section covers the effects of having no to-do list in your day-to-day life.

How Your Life would be Without a To-Do List

Life, by nature, is chaotic in itself. This is further complicated by the demands and complexities of the modern way of living.

With the mountain of tasks that you must accomplish day by day, things can quickly become overwhelming. When this builds up, the amount of stress in your life will increase exponentially.

Many experts recommend the usage of a to-do list to manage one's activities and responsibilities better. However, some people find it hard to pick this up as a habit.

Studies show that without a to-do list, an individual's level of productivity significantly drops down. You may also experience the following scenarios when you do not create a to-do list of your own:

- jumping from one task to another, thus decreasing your efficiency in finishing up your tasks;

- missing out on important deadlines because you forgot that you have to do it in the first place;

- being vulnerable to potential distractions around you;

- struggling to achieve a balance between your home life, your work life, and social life, among others;

- having no sense of direction at all especially when it comes to what you should be doing next; and

- lacking the feeling of accomplishment by the end of the day.

To resolve these problems, you should try incorporating the creation of a to-do list in your daily habits.

How a To-Do List Helps with Overthinking

One of the most significant negative effects of overthinking is analysis paralysis. This means that you become stuck in your mind, mulling over the same issue over and over again, without anything to show for it. This then leaves you with little to no time and energy to act and carry out your other tasks.

A to-do list can help you overcome this by keeping you focused and on track with what truly matters. Aside from boosting your productivity, it may also be beneficial to you in psychological terms.

According to researchers, a to-do list can:

- give you the motivation to get things done;
- prevents you from being distracted by your irrelevant thoughts and other unnecessary elements from your environment;
- prevents you from doing unnecessary repetitive behaviors;
- break down complicated tasks that may bring about feelings of anxiety and worry about failing to accomplish the said task;
- improve your pacing, and therefore decrease your stress level;
- relieve you of the pressure to finish everything all at once; and
- relieve you of the worry that you have forgotten to do something important.

Ultimately, a to-do list can also make you feel happy and satisfied. A listing with all the items crossed out serves as proof that your day has been quite productive. You will be able to fight off any feelings of doubt, especially those of self-worth and self-confidence. As such, your mind will have no reason to devolve into an endless spiral of anxiety, negative thoughts, and worry.

Maintain a To-Do List & Stick to it

Many people who do not—and can not—maintain a to-do list view it as a burden. They think of it as a list of chores to do and deadlines to meet. Over time, this perception prevents them from making a habit out of creating and managing a to-do list.

Some people are natural at keeping things organized and on track. However, for those who are not born or conditioned to do so, here are some effective tips that will allow you to maintain and stick to your to-do list:

- Associate your to-do list with positive thoughts and feelings.

    This is the first thing you must do to incorporate a to-do list in your daily life successfully. Remind yourself of the practical benefits of keeping one. Try to recall how good it feels whenever you get to cross something off your list. By doing this, your brain will be conditioned to put things in your to-do list to get it done and crossed off.

- Write the list for the benefit of the future.

    You might not immediately realize the advantages of maintaining a good to-do list, but your future self would appreciate your efforts. No matter how good you are at remembering things, life may throw you a curveball at any moment.

    This may leave you scrambling for direction and information. A to-do list that contains all the important details that you must keep in mind would be a lifeline during those challenging times.

- Categorize the items on your list, depending on their importance and your personal preference.

    Many people skip the process of categorizing the items on the to-do list. This is an important step to make because it improves your chances of getting things done. Through this, you would be able to prioritize your tasks better.

One way to categorize your list is by arranging it according to what must be done, and what would be nice to do if you have the extra time. By doing so, you would not miss out on the all-too-important deadlines in your life. It will also remind you of the things you can do with your time, thus saving you from having to rack your head for something to do.

- Accept the fact that to-do lists are changeable.

  Remember, a to-do list is only a tool. Its contents are not rules or demands that you must follow at all costs. Sometimes, you have to change the items in your list to suit your current needs.

  Starting anew is perfectly alright. It shows that you flexible enough to roll with the punches. By learning how to adjust yourself and your to-do list, you will be able to better deal with the stress and anxiety triggers that may come your way.

- Treat your to-do list as a symbol of your accomplishments.

  Conquering your to-do list requires a lot of time and effort. Therefore, it is normal to feel proud about finishing a task in your to-do list.

Similar to assigning positive feelings to your list, thinking of it as a record of your wins for the day will help you stick to this habit.

This will also do wonders for your mental health. Anxiety, negative thoughts, and worries will have little to no place left in your head when it is filled with your accomplishments for the day.

Now that you understand the importance of having a to-do list and how maintaining one can drastically simplify any feelings of anxiety, negative thoughts and worries you could have, it is also important to know how to create an effective to-do list.

Creating an Effective To-Do List

Some rush through the process of creating a list, thus giving them a one-word outline that vaguely describes what they must do. As a result, they cannot follow through the listed tasks, which then leaves them an impression that to-do lists simply do not work for them.

To help you write an effective to-do list that WORKS for you, follow these quick and easy steps:

1. **List down three tasks, at most.**

A shorter list containing the most important tasks that you must accomplish would allow you to get a sense of accomplishment by the end of the day.

2. **Make each task actionable.**

   You can do this by using an active voice rather than simply indicating the outcome that you want to accomplish. For example, instead of listing down "detergent" in your list, you should write "go to the grocery store and buy detergent."

   The first part of the suggested statement may sound obvious and unnecessary to you. However, keep in mind that the more complicated the task, the more helpful it is to include these small details into your to-do list.

3. **Assign the priority level for each task.**

   You may ask yourself which of these tasks would make you feel most accomplished. Your answer would then have to go to the top of your to-do list (priority list) with a "high", "mid", or "low" label depending on their relative urgency to you.

4. **Write down the rest of your tasks in a separate sheet or file (overflow list).**

They should go to another queue, so that you can focus on what matters. Since the top three tasks are considered as significant items, they may also take up a lot of your time. Therefore, keeping the other tasks in a different list would keep you from feeling overwhelmed.

Ideally, you should store this where it is accessible but away from your sight. This would enable you to refer to the overflow list when you have run out of things to do in your priority list.

5. **Make your priority to-do list visible.**

    You may transfer them in small post-it notes that you can stick in a location that you frequently see or go to, such as the refrigerator door. If you prefer to add more details, you may opt to use index cards instead.

6. **View each task one at a time.**

    Many people feel overwhelmed whenever they see a list of things that they must do. To prevent this from turning into a negative feeling, you can impose viewing limits upon yourself.

    There are certain task management apps, such as the "Todoist" and "Omnifocus", that allow their users this viewing option. However, if you are using post-it notes or index cards, then you can just simply stack them over one another so that you can only see the topmost item in your list.

7. **Record the status of your task**

Recording the status of your task whether accomplished or not makes you accountable. It makes you have a deeper reflection on the position of your commitment to fulfilling your tasks for the day. It makes you ponder on how you can improve on your level of accomplishment and also gives you a sense of refocus to ensuring that unaccomplished tasks are executed and taken off your to-do list as quickly as possible.

===========**Break in Transmission**========

Permit me to take a brief pause right here to ask for a favor. If you have found the first few chapters of this book insightful and helpful to you, kindly leave an honest review on amazon. Reviews encourage other readers to give independent authors like myself a chance to be heard. Trust me, it sure helps. To leave a review, simply type this link https://amzn.to/357b84s

into your web browser if you're in the US or https://amzn.to/34afNBg if you're in the UK.

Thank you!

Case Study

Despite Amy's effort to research about potential strategies, she felt like she was not making much progress on this. Her main problem was that due to the overwhelming amount of information she had amassed, she was not entirely sure where to start. She also kept jumping from one strategy to another, thus leaving her a pile of unfinished tasks.

To resolve this, Amy followed the advice of her best friend, Danny, to make a to-do list. Since this is incredibly personal, she downloaded a task management app on her phone, where she can privately store her to-do list.

Amy also decided to create one list per recurring issue that she had identified earlier. In that way, she would know if she had done any action in resolving the said issues. Using the app, she assigned the priority levels and set up reminders that will notify her now and then of what she should be doing.

After a week of using the to-do list, Amy finally felt like she was back on track with her personal project to stop overthinking.

Practice Test

Create your own to-do list for each day or as required using the format below.

For the "Priority Level", assign each task a "high", "mid", or "low" label depending on their relative urgency to you.

Use the "Status" column the following day to indicate whether or not you have accomplished your tasks.

Task #	Task	Priority Level	Status

Carry out the task listed in the table you have made. On the following day, answer the following questions based on your experience:

- How many tasks have you accomplished?
- How did you feel when you accomplished a task?
- How many tasks have you not accomplished?
- How do you feel now that you have not accomplished a task from yesterday?
- How do you think you can improve upon your level of accomplishment?

Chapter 5

Live a Minimalist Lifestyle

"The secret of happiness, you see, is not found in seeking more, but in developing the capacity to enjoy less."

—Socrates

What is Minimalism?

Many people associate minimalism with stark white walls and sparsely furnished rooms. However, that aspect is only one aspect of minimalism—one that is done out of the personal preference of the individual.

Lifestyle experts consider minimalism as a way of life that encourages intentionality, simplicity, and clarity among its followers. Its applications are not only limited to the home, but also other important aspects of life, such as your relationships, career, and digital presence.

Minimalism promotes the recognition of the value of the things you keep and the people you interact with.

As a result, anything that does not fit with your goals and purpose in life is discarded or avoided.

Some people misunderstand minimalism by equating "less" with "none." However, this assumption does not align with the basic principles of this movement. Minimalists are allowed to keep things with sentimental value—even though the said things do not serve any other function whatsoever. As long as something brings value to your life, then you may choose to keep it with you.

Embracing minimalism may require significant changes in your current lifestyle. It is well worth doing, given the benefits, it brings, especially for the wellness of your mental health.

Benefits of a Minimalist Lifestyle?

A minimalist lifestyle is considered as the complete opposite of a life riddled with anxiety.

Anxiety is characterized by excessive worrying, overthinking, and high levels of stress. As a result, you will lose focus on what you should be doing. You become easily overwhelmed by your responsibilities, negative thoughts, and fears.

This condition is further exacerbated by a cluttered space. It is difficult to relax and be calm in an environment filled with unnecessary and disorganized things.

On the other hand, minimalism promotes a clear focus on the things that matter in life. Therefore, you may be able to pursue your goals and function well without giving in to the distractions around you.

When you adopt a minimalist lifestyle, you will gradually be freed from the rush and demands of the modern way of living. Since you have to disengage from non-value adding activities, you will have more time to pursue the things that you want to do in your life. You may also use this time to improve the quality of relationships that you have with the people around you.

To reap the benefits of a minimalist life, you need to learn how you can incorporate its principles into various aspects of your life. To guide you through this, given below are the essential tips for beginners.

How to Apply Minimalism in Your Everyday Life

- Home

The goal when reducing the clutter in your home is to assess whether or not an item adds value to your home or has a value to you. Based on your assessment, you may categorize each item according to these categories:

- o For keeping
- o For donation
- o For selling
- o For disposal

Saving an item may mean that it has practical use in your home, or that it has a sentimental value that makes you want to cherish it. An item may also possess both qualities, like a set of hand towels that you have received as a gift from your mother.

If you choose to donate an item, it is best to select a local organization that helps individuals who may find a use for your item. You may also consider donating them to thrift stores that would sell the item to those in need.

Selling can either be done by holding a garage sale, or by posting it on online platforms.

Through this, you will be able to convert the item into something more useful to you.

Disposing of the items that have no use or no sentimental value to you can be beneficial for your overall wellness. You would typically feel a sense of accomplishment because you have attained your goal for this project. The process itself can also relieve you of stress and anxiety since the items may be contributing to the negative thoughts and feelings that you have.

For this process to be institutionalized within you, it is advisable to make a schedule for this. How frequent you do it depends on your preference. What matters is that you will allot a specific time dedicated to this activity.

- Workplace

    Since your personal space at work is most likely limited only to your workstation, then this is the best starting point. You may begin by removing all items from your desk. Wipe it clean, and remove any stains, if there are any.

    Then, sort through your stuff by assigning their respective value to your work. Anything that does not serve any purpose to your current responsibilities and projects should either be archived somewhere else or discarded properly.

Once you are done, rearrange the things you have identified as essential back on your desk. Dispose of any remaining clutter to keep your workspace clean and organized.

To prevent you from overthinking, which things will be kept and which will be discarded, set a timer to 15 minutes only. By sticking to the time limit, your mind will be forced to focus on your objectives.

You may repeat this process every week, or whenever you notice clutter piling up in your workspace again.

- Relationships (Romantic & Friendship)

    By applying minimalism to your relationships, you will be able to finally move on from the painful experiences you have had in the past and replace that emptied space with good memories that you will have with your new relationships.

    To do this, you must first let go of the past. Acknowledge the mistakes that you have made and move forward while bringing along only the lessons you have learned from them.

Then, apply the principle of "less is more" in terms of determining the relationships that you want to add and keep in your life. You don't need hundreds of acquaintances when you can have a handful of true friends who have your back no matter what.

- Digital Life

    Digital minimalism aims to ensure that our use of technology is intentional and kept at the barest minimum. It is motivated by the fact that intentionally doing away with digital noise, and optimizing your use of the available digital tools that are important, can tremendously improve the quality of your life.

    In this technologically advanced age, we often get bogged down with lots of digital distractions, which could come in different forms that most times cause us to lose ourselves in the process, leading to an out of control feeling of anxieties, negative thoughts and worries.

To have better control of your thoughts, there are several digital minimalist practices that you can apply to simplify your digital and online presence to gain better control of your thoughts, a few of which I would touch on below.

- o Simplifying your Digital Files and Emails

Clutter can also pile up in your files and emails. This can come in various forms, such as an overflowing inbox, or a maxed-out hard drive. Much like physical clutter, these can contribute to your stress level and anxiety.

To apply minimalism to your files and emails, you first have to go through each of your digital files and emails. Delete those that are not important, and categorize those that you will keep. To prevent the mistake of deleting an important file, it is best to save a back-up copy before commencing this activity.

It is easy to put this off for another time, especially since it is not as pressing as your other tasks. However, you have to give time for this, even in small 10-minute bursts throughout the week. By doing this, you will be able to clean up your files and rearrange them in an orderly fashion.

Scheduling this activity regularly would also keep everything manageable for a longer period. A once-a-week backup and cleanup of your digital files and emails should be sufficient enough in most cases.

- Simplifying Usage of Social Media

Social media is a wonderful yet noisy place, which attributes to one of the major sources of anxiety, negative thoughts, and worries. If you fail to use it wisely, you would most likely be caught up with the clutter it freely gives and ending up in rabbit holes. For example, people who visit Facebook regularly may experience a change of mood to somewhat negative because you get caught up comparing your life with others you see on Facebook who appear successful, beautiful, and happy.

Although social media has helped in making useful professional connections easier such as LinkedIn, even at that, you might feel professional anxiety when your peers are making waves in their careers and life in general. Hence, it has become increasingly important to minimize your usage of social media to keep your mental health in check.

To keep your thoughts in check, you need to realize that most people who put up great posts on social media have a normal life just like you but only put the good stuff they want you to see, leaving out the not so good things about their lives— some people put up a "fake it until you make it" post. The bottom line here is social media isn't real life, and you simply have to take whatever you see on social media with little or better still no interest and go out there in the real world and live your best life.

You can also control what you see on social media. Simply unfriend and unfollow anyone whose posts or feeds are both distracting and of no value to your life. If this still doesn't help, then deactivate your social media accounts and delete the social media app from your phone. Trust me; you'll survive only if you make it an intentional decision. Your mental health comes first before any other thing.

Case Study

One of the potential strategies that Amy was considering is adopting a minimalistic lifestyle. Before trying it out, she decided to analyze first how she could apply it to the key areas in her life. Given that her triggers are work-related, she opted to focus on that during this trial phase.

Booting up her work laptop, Amy looked through her files and inbox to check their current status. She frequently did not take the time to sort her documents into the right folders properly. Most of them are just there on her desktop. Her inbox was also filled with unread messages from the various sites that she had subscribed to while she was conducting her research.

Applying the principles of minimalism, Amy sorted, deleted, and categorized all of her files and emails, over one week. She also unsubscribed from any previously joined mailing list she no longer needed that contributed to the overflow in her inbox. By the end of it, she felt a sense of calm whenever she saw how organized her files and emails are.

To maintain this, she added in her to-do list a regular cleanup of both her files and inbox.

Practice Test

Try to apply the guidelines given earlier in this chapter regarding the reduction of clutter in your digital files. Makes sure to save a backup of your files and emails first before proceeding with this exercise.

After doing this activity, answer the following questions based on your experience:

- How do you feel after completing this exercise?

Do you think you can create a habit out of this? Why or why not?

Chapter 6

Get Rid of the Past and Bad Relationships

"Letting go doesn't mean that you don't care about someone anymore. It's just realizing that the only person you really have control over is yourself."

— Deborah Reber

Get Unstuck from Your Ugly Memories

Letting go of the past is easier said than done. However, people are hardwired to hold on to things that feel familiar and comforting. Even when it is essentially based on a negative experience, the human mind tends to romanticize certain aspects of the past.

Some people use their past as an excuse and basis for the decisions they are making now. For example, Glenn had a nasty argument with his former high school friend, Karen. As a result, he decided to burn bridges between her and his other friends in high school, thinking that he had already outgrown them at this point in his life.

This example shows how dangerous the past can be to your present and future. The kind of memories you keep shapes your current path and controls the direction that you are heading to.

Therefore, if you keep holding on to the past, especially to your negative experiences, then expect misery and loneliness to be your perennial companions in life.

To realign your focus towards a more optimistic and fulfilling future, then you have to learn how to let go of your past. This involves all the mistakes you have made, and the bad decisions that continue to haunt you.

Past relationships are usually riddled with mistakes and bad decisions. Yet, they are often the hardest things to let go of from your past. No matter how badly it ended, people tend to hold on to the experiences and feelings they have had with the former partners.

To free yourself from these memories, you have to take a proactive approach. Time will not simply heal your wounds if you keep prodding at them. You need to actively find ways to sever the ties that keep you from accepting the past and moving on.

Acknowledging the existence of a problem triggers the need for a solution. Therefore, the first step you need to take is recognizing a bad relationship for what it is.

How You Can Identify a Bad Relationship

Many people find it hard to recognize if they are in a bad relationship or not. Some have been conditioned to accept unhealthy expressions of love as normal, while others make up excuses for their partner's flaws. People who feel like they are too deep in their relationship tend to turn a blind on the glaring signs around them.

Some relationship issues can be passed off as mere quirks that you can learn to accept overtime. However, there are serious relationship problems that can make or break a couple.

To help you identify the red flags of a bad relationship, here is a list of the signs that you need to look out for:

- You feel like you have to change yourself to better suit your partner.

  It is perfectly alright to try out new hobbies that your partner has, just to see if you would also enjoy doing them. It is also fine to switch things up in your life, for the benefit of your growth and development as a person.

This becomes a serious issue if you feel like the current version of you would not meet the expectations of your partner. If you find yourself changing the way you normally dress, or if you start changing your opinions and values according to your partner's thoughts and feelings, then your relationship with him/her has crossed the line of what is acceptable and what is not.

- You have to defend your partner to family members and friends.

Not everyone has to like your partner, but it is alarming when no one among your family and friends like him/her. If they are all uncomfortable with your relationship, then it may be a sign that you have to take a better look at it.

- Your partner frequently criticizes you, even when said criticism had been expressed as a joke.

By doing this, your partner is putting you down in a passive-aggressive manner. Over time, these criticisms will chip away your self-confidence, which can then lead to feelings of anxiety, negative thoughts, and worries about the future of your relationship with him/her.

- You always find yourself wondering what your partner is doing whenever you are not with him/her.

If your gut is telling you that something is off, then you should first communicate with your partner about your doubts and insecurities. If he/she refuses to engage with you on this, then, more often than not, there is something else going on that could significantly affect your relationship with them.

Tolerating this kind of relationship can be tiresome, especially since it will lead you to overthink things between the two of you.

- Your partner usually makes big decisions for both of you and without consulting you beforehand.

Re-evaluate your relationship if your partner is the only one calling all the shots. It does not have to be as big as buying a house for both of you without consulting you beforehand. Going to events alone that he/she wants to go to reflects the uneven balance of power between the two of you.

- Sometimes, you need to be alone for a moment, but your partner refuses to give you space.

Self-care is important whether or not you are in a relationship. Wanting some time alone does not mean that you have a problem with your partner. If your partner does not understand that, even after you have explained your reasons to him/her, then your boundaries are being ignored. That is not a good sign because it may develop further into control issues later on.

- You feel responsible for the happiness of your partner.

If your partner relies on you and only you to be happy, then it can cause an imbalance in your mental and emotional state. For example, your partner blames you whenever he/she is upset or angry. Moreover, he/she expects you to remedy the situation or change yourself to make them feel better.

Such a situation can put a lot of strain on you mentally and emotionally. Feeling like you have to walk on eggshells around them, just to keep them happy, is a sign that you are in a toxic relationship.

- Your partner controls or at least try to control what you do and who you spend time with.

Many relationship experts consider this as the biggest red flag that you should look out for. If your partner wants to control your finances, your relationships with other people, or even your appearance, then you should take a step back from him/her. Take a serious look at your relationship, and communicate your concerns about his/her control issues over you. How they respond to this would determine whether or not the relationship is worth saving.

- You ask yourself if you are in a bad relationship.

Ignoring the significance of this question can be a source of regret for you later. The simple fact that you are wondering about this is a sign that something is off about your relationship with him/her.

Rather than overthink the answer to this question, it is best to take a more proactive approach. Talk to your partner and see if things can still be changed for the better. If not, then you should get out of that relationship before you get hurt any further.

Though these signs are mainly for romantic relationships, most of these red flags are also applicable to other types of relationships that you have in your life. For instance, having an overly dependent friend can too be taxing for your wellbeing. A controlling family member can be just as toxic as a controlling partner.

Evaluate all the relationships in your life, and see if any of them are leading you to engage in overthinking, or causing you to feel anxiety. Once you have accepted the fact that there is a problem, then it will be easier for you to find the motivation to move on with your life without them.

Let Go of Certain People

Now that you can identify the relationships that are holding you back, you may now start working on how to let go of them. By doing so, you would also leave more space in your life for positive people who share similar interests, values, and outlook in life as you have.

It is highly likely that you have an idea of what kind of relationships you want to have— about the quality of your friends you want or the characteristics you expect of your significant other. Normally, you would avoid people who bring negativity and distractions along with them. If your goal in life is to be happy and free from your worries, then why would you choose to be with someone who makes you feel anxious?

It may sound obvious to you now, but the fact is, many people fail to let go of these types of people in their life. The insecurities that one possesses, as well as the fear of ending up all alone in life, may prevent common sense from taking over. As a result, bad relationships persist, and so do negative thoughts and feelings that one might have.

Be more selective of your relationships since they usually have more influence over your thoughts and actions than you realize. Surround yourself with people who prefer seeing the brighter things in life, rather than those who like to sulk and mope around. Find someone who shares your dreams, so that you can have a worthy companion while you are on your way to attaining them.

Tips to Shake Off Bad Relationships from Your Life

To help you move on from the relationships you have identified as problematic, here are three important tips that you can apply to get rid of the toxic people in your life finally:

- Set and stick to your boundaries.

    Establish clear guidelines on how you will move on and impose them upon yourself. Even if they try to break through the walls you have put up around yourself, keep them up no matter what.

    If you have told yourself that you will stop all forms of communication with them, then do not respond to their texts and calls. Block them from your phone and social media accounts. Do not be tempted to check in on them because you have decided that you are already done with them.

- Stop being overly accommodating to their needs and wants.

    Toxic people will try to take advantage of whatever fondness and concern that you have for them. Being too nice can be detrimental to your progress in moving on from the relationship.

You do not have to be mean to them, however. Just stop trying to make them feel better about the end of your relationship. You are not responsible for their happiness.

- Be firm with your decision.

   Keep in mind that the decision you have made is based on significant reasons to move on from the relationship. If you have trouble remembering them, write them down in your journal. By doing so, you will be able to remind yourself why you need to be firm with your decision, especially when the person you have removed from your life tries to get back in.

   In the case of toxic family members, it can be hard to break off the relationship completely. For such breakups, the best thing you can do is to impose clear limitations on your future interactions with them.

I would share a personal experience on this subject. I once had a colleague when I was still in the business of the 9-5 work-life, who was more of a friend than a colleague. We would get along happily at work. Then all of a sudden, on one fateful regular workday, her attitude toward me changed. It is like she never knew me or we have never met. I made many attempts to figure out what happened or why she was acting so cold around me and indifferent toward me, but all proved to be unsuccessful. I felt it was unfair to be treated so cold, given our friendly history. The thought of bumping into her during work and getting those negative vibes from her sure gave me cold feet, made me anxious, triggered this worry and overthinking loop of what to do or not to do whenever our paths crossed. I felt her opinion of me mattered, and this was taking a toll on my health, my relationship with other colleagues, and, to some extent, on my work. I quickly realized the negative impact of her attitude toward me on my mental state. Then I decided I had had enough of her shenanigans. No more of such was I taking from her, and no more would she cause me to be anxious and worried.

What did I do?

Your guess is as good as my response.

I decided I was going to ignore her attitude toward me, never caring what she thought of me or her opinions about me, stop any further unwarranted communication with her that isn't work-related, and continued living and working like she never existed — literally speaking. That is not to say I disrespected her in any way when doing any of these, but I was simply numb to her presence around me, and sure, this felt good, and I had a great sense of relief from having to be anxious when we bumped into each other.

The bottom line is, the more time you spend away from the people you are trying to get rid of, the better your chances of completely moving on. The time that will be freed up by your breakup can be spent on doing things for yourself or seeking other people who would infuse more positivity into your life.

Let go of those who bring you misery and welcome those who will bring you happiness.

Let's find out how Amy was able to handle a similar situation like mine with her colleagues.

Case Study

Another source of Amy's anxiety is her work colleagues. She was one of the recent additions to the team, so she still had not yet figured out their personalities and work ethics.

Amy's main problem with some of them is the unsolicited comments about her style of teaching and the way she dressed up for work. Due to her anxiety, she had never communicated with them how she felt upon hearing those comments. She was particularly worried that doing so would only alienate her further from them.

Since she had taken up the initiative to stop engaging in overthinking, Amy mustered up the courage to strike up a conversation with Dorothy, one of the teachers who had been pretty vocal about her opinions of her.

During their conversation, Amy realized that the comments were mostly rooted in the generational gap that existed between the two of them. Before ending the conversation, Amy had asked Dorothy to refrain from making comments about her work and her appearance, especially in front of other teachers and students.

Dorothy promised that she would stop, but after two days, Amy had overheard Dorothy talking about her again. This time, her colleague was complaining about the way Amy had confronted her the other day.

Despite feeling hurt, Amy decided to walk away for now. She needed to cool her head down before forming up a plan to resolve this issue.

N.B: To find out how Amy eventually handled the situation with her colleagues, kindly read through to the last chapter.

Practice Test

Based on the points that you have learned in this chapter, answer the following questions about Amy's problem with some of her colleagues:

- Do you think Amy should have confronted Dorothy about the comments on Amy's teaching style and appearance? Why or why not?

- Does Amy's work relationship with Dorothy show any of the warning signs of a bad relationship? Please specify the red flags that you are seeing in their relationship as colleagues.

- If you were in Amy's shoes, how would you treat Dorothy after the recent incident?

Chapter 7

Pursue Your Goals

"I don't focus on what I'm up against. I focus on my goals, and I try to ignore the rest."

— Venus Williams

Pursuing your goals is most often easier said than done. The thought of having to take that big step to change your career path or quitting your job to start and own your own business, write and publish that long-overdue book or books you keep pushing off all in a bid to pursue your goals can be overwhelming, scary and harder to follow through — not necessarily because they are impossible to accomplish, but because they inherently come with an excessive amount of anxieties, negative thoughts, and worries:

- That a million things could go wrong if you embark on this journey.
- That you "may" fail.
- Of what people will think and so on.

It is one thing to set a goal to discontinue the use of certain social media apps on your phone or the internet and fall flat of it, and it is another thing entirely to pursue your life dream only to realize it has been nothing more of a pipe-dream.

Overcoming the feeling of anxieties, negative thoughts, and worries to go after your goals may not be easy, but it is possible, absolutely possible. And I will show you how you can achieve this and be accountable to it in the subsequent paragraphs. One thing is for sure and certain, pursuing your goals vis-à-vis your passions, are one of the most gratifying and fulfilling feelings you could ever wish for. It automatically gives you a heightened sense of purpose, accomplishment, peace, and happiness. You can take this to the bank.

To get started on pursuing your goals, permit me to hold you by your hand as I take the lead (*laughs*).

Discover Your Vocation

Starting in early childhood, parents, teachers, and maybe even friends have asked you this question: what do you want to be when you grow up? Up to your teenage years, plans in life often tend to be vague yet grand. The pressure usually begins to mount during the latter part, when people are about to choose the degree they will pursue in the university, or when they are trying to start a career out of their gained knowledge, talents, and skills.

Therein lies the problem because many people tend to go with what feels okay at the moment. As a result, they switch majors or jobs within the first few couples of years after they have made a decision.

There is nothing wrong with seeking your passions by trying out different things. However, since most people do not yet have a concrete idea of what they want to achieve in life, their decisions to go for a degree or a job are mostly based on what they are trying to avoid—not what they want to do. For instance, they do not want to be stuck in a mundane 9-to-5 job—something like what their fathers and mothers used to do.

That is a shaky foundation for something that you will be doing for around forty years of your life. Having the answer to what you want to be when you grow up is the ideal basis for this kind of decision. However, if that is too hard for you to answer, even now that you are in your adulthood, then perhaps the question that you should be asking yourself is this: what is your vocation?

If you are familiar with the concept of a vocation, here is how it compares to the other two perspectives that one may have about work:

- Job

    A job is a simple means to an end. By doing your job, you will get a paycheck. That paycheck is needed for your day-to-day expenses, for supporting your family, and for paying rent—which is where most of the paycheck typically goes.

    People with jobs look forward to breaks from their work, especially extended ones where they can take a vacation. Even though their jobs are not horrible or completely mundane, whatever they do for work offers little to no life satisfaction at all.

- Career

    People with careers get their satisfaction not from their work itself, but from the possible advancements that they can make by being good at what they do. They are excited about moving up through the ranks, earning a higher salary, and getting better benefits.

As such, careerists do not find it hard to put in extra time to their day-to-day work. They are eager to move up, so they opt to work as hard as they can. However, when the opportunity to move upward is taken away, or when they have nowhere else to go in the field of work they have chosen, then their satisfaction dives down, thus turning their enthusiasm into frustration and disappointment.

- Vocation

    Your calling or vocation refers to the work you do just for its own sake. You will know it is a vocation when you almost feel like you would still happily do the work even if you do not get paid for it. It would make you think that this is exactly what you are meant to do.

    Though vocations have a reputation for being low-paying work, that only holds true during the start. Once you have established yourself and your passion has translated into the quality of work that you do, then you will receive your due, usually many times over. The money and prestige that you can get by finding and applying your vocation, however, are peripheral only to the ultimate benefit that you can get from it.

Your calling allows you to pursue your passions in life in a gratifying way. The work you do makes you feel that you are contributing to a greater good that goes beyond your personal welfare. Furthermore, applying a vocation allows you to make use of special gifts and talents.

Comparing these three, those who work for a job feels the least happiness and satisfaction in life. This is followed by people with a career, while those who have found and followed their calling tend to be the happiest and most satisfied with what they do.

Such an observation is not surprising because a vocation does not only affect your work life. It reflects your true purpose in life. When you find your calling, you will notice the effects in profound ways. Your life will be filled with joy and fulfilment.

People who have not found their vocation yet often find themselves wondering if what they are doing now is what they would want to be doing for the rest of their lives. A great weight will build up in their chest as time goes by.

Discovering your true calling in life is not something that you would usually stumble upon. You may be doing a job that utilizes your talent, but it does fulfil you because the purpose is not related to your passion. You may also be working in a field close to your passions, but the employer does not allow you to make significant contributions using your talent. Neither of these scenarios is ideal for your pursuit of fulfilment from your work.

Therefore, to find your true vocation, you need to recognize not only your skills and talents but also your passions in life.

What Motivates You? – Your Passions

Discovering your passion is not as hard as you think it is. The answer, however, is critical in determining what you want to do in life. This is not limited to those who are just about to enter the university or the workforce. It is also a common problem among those who feel bored, lost, or unfulfilled with their current jobs.

To figure out what truly motivates you, here are some suggestions that you can try out for yourself.

- Answer these three questions.
    - Which topic can you read a thousand books about without getting bored out of your mind?

- What is the one thing that you do not mind doing for a whole decade without getting paid?

- How would you spend your time if you are so financially secure that you do not have to work for a living?

If your answers to these questions have a common theme at the very least, then that is likely your passion in life.

- Visualize your dream job.

Imagine yourself waking up in the morning even before your alarm has gone off. You dress up quickly, not because you are running late but because you are excited to go to work. The sun is shining brightly outside, and you take a step outside your home. Where are you heading to? What are you about to do when you get to work?

Your passions may be found with the help of your subconscious mind. Let your imagination run free to discover what lies beneath your doubt, worries, and insecurities.

- Recall what you loved doing when you were just a kid.

Did you enjoy drawing pictures or baking cookies with your mom? Do you want to continue doing that now that you are an adult? What are your hobbies that started when you were young and persists to be an interest up to this day? Make these memories as your reference on what you would want to do now.

- Ask your family and close friends for advice.

    You do not have to shoulder everything when trying to discover your passions in life. The people who know you best might have some important inputs that can lead you to the right answer.

    Do not put them on the spot, however. Let them think about it for some time. This will ensure that what you are getting from them is something worthy of serious consideration.

Note Down Your Life Goals

Now that you have a better idea of what you want to achieve, it is best to write them down in your journal.

According to experts, tangibly recording them improves one's odds in transforming them into reality.

The simple act of documenting your goals prompts the subconscious mind to begin thinking of them as opportunities. This is not possible if you are merely thinking of your goals because the brain handles so many things all at once that your goals might be completely overlooked and forgotten.

To start building a habit of noting down your life goals, here is an exercise that you should try doing every morning for the following seven days. In a journal, write down your goals for each important aspect of your life. You can add it to the list below.

- Personal health
- Relationships
- Vocation

Go beyond what you think you can have, or what seems possible at this moment in your life. Instead, write down goals that you want to achieve, regardless of how grand or ambitious it may sound to you right now.

Though this exercise may seem simple, it will enable you to:

- Achieve a higher clarity about your life goals; and
- Recognize the value of opportunities that come your way based on how they would help you achieve your goals.

It is not enough, however, to simply know what you want to do. You also need to gain and sustain the drive to pursue them relentlessly, despite the challenges, anxieties, and worries that you might face along the way. This is how your passions in life can enhance your strategies to achieve your goals.

Connect Goals to Passions and Prioritize Them

You need to make time for your passions since they will lead you to your true purpose in life. To do so, you need to focus on them by centering your goals around your passions in life.

Since you are motivated to pursue what you love, then you would also be more driven to push past the challenges and achieve your goals.

In an ideal world, you will attain whatever you have set your mind to achieve. However, in reality, you can only do so much at a time, no matter how motivated you are.

You must, therefore, learn how to prioritize the important life goals that you have on your list.

To do so, here are some guide questions that can help you set your priorities. Answer them truthfully to come up with a list of passion-driven goals that you need to prioritize. It is best to write down your answers in your journal so that you can reflect on them after answering these questions.

- Which of your goals do you think of the most?
- Which of your goals would energize you the most once you have committed to them?
- Which goal would make you feel the proudest once you have accomplished it?
- Which goal would have personal importance to you for the rest of your life?
- Which of your goals is completely aligned with your values?
- Which of your goals is within the bounds of your control and not entirely dependent on your current circumstance or some other person?

Since you have written down your responses, you can review them to gain insight into what your priorities should be. Do not force yourself, though. Take your time. You may even re-do the questions if you are not satisfied with what you can glean off of them.

Once you have assigned priorities to your goals, then you are now ready to proceed in making them more manageable.

Set S.M.A.R.T. Goals

This refers to a goal-setting strategy that translates vaguely written goals into more defined and actionable items. Through this, you would be able to clarify what you should be doing, when you should accomplish it, and how you would know if you have successfully attained them.

The acronym S.M.A.R.T. stands for:

- Specific

  Your goal should be clearly stated so that you would know exactly what you are trying to achieve.

- Measurable

  Through this, you will be able to monitor your progress and stay focused on meeting your projected timeline. As you draw closer to your goal, you would also feel more motivated to push through until the end of the line.

- Achievable

    A goal has to be based on your reality so that you may have a chance to achieve it. However, do not set your goal so low because it will negatively affect your motivation and sense of fulfillment. The sweet spot is somewhere a bit further than your comfort zone. It should stretch you a bit, but not too much that it may strain you.

- Relevant

    This would ensure that the goal you are pursuing is significant to you. Otherwise, you might lose your drive eventually, thus wasting whatever time, effort, and resources that you have already exerted to achieve the said goal.

- Time-Bound

    A goal needs a due date to be effective. Otherwise, you would not be able to impose your priorities well.

How to Set S.M.A.R.T. Goals that WORKS!

To help you effectively apply the principles of S.M.A.R.T. to your goals, here are some essential questions you should answer.

- Specific

    You may define your goal in great detail by answering the 5 "W" questions:

    o What do you want to achieve?

    o Why is this goal significant to you?

    o Who are the people involved in achieving this goal?

    o Where is it going to take place?

    o Which of your resources and limitations would apply to this goal?

- Measurable

    You may assess the measurability of your goal if it addresses the following questions:

    o How many/much _____ do you need to achieve your goal?

    o How will you know if you have already achieved your goal?

- Achievable

    To make your goal attainable, answer the following guide questions:

    o What strategy/strategies are you going to use to accomplish your goal?

    o How realistic is your goal against your current personal limitations (i.e., skills, talents, financial status, etc.)?

- Relevant

    A goal is relevant to you if you can answer "yes" to the following questions:

    o Is the goal worth your time, effort, and resources?

    o Is it the right time to pursue this goal?

    o Is it aligned with your other goals and needs in life?

- Time-Bound

    You can establish the timeline for your goal by answering these questions:

    o When do you need to accomplish this goal?

- What can you do today/___ week from now/___ month from now/___ year from now to get closer to your goal?

To make your S.M.A.R.T. goals even more effective, you should positively construct them. For example, rather than saying, "Do not skip breakfast," you should say, "Eat a healthy and balanced meal during breakfast time every day."

You should also reflect upon your list of S.M.A.R.T. goals regularly. Set a schedule for your reviews and personal evaluations. This will help you keep your list up-to-date vis-à-vis your current situation and what you have achieved so far.

If you have diligently followed through with this very chapter, I believe you should have been able to gain an enormous amount of inner strength and insights that have not only helped you to discover your vocation (if you haven't before now) but to also help you in pursuing your goals to the finish line without having to feel any form of anxiety, negative thought or worry of not pulling through.

Case Study

Aside from making to-do lists, Amy had also decided to set effective goals that will ultimately lead her to stop overthinking on how to go about pursuing and achieving her goals. To do this, she applied the principles of S.M.A.R.T. goals.

Using her list of recurring triggers as her basis, Amy formed goals for the successful resolution of each trigger. For example, under the trigger prompted by her upcoming performance appraisal, she wrote down this goal:

"At least one week before the performance appraisal, conduct a dry run of the proposed lesson plan to be used for the evaluation with a different set of students."

Practice Test

Analyze Amy's sub-goal to ace the performance appraisal vis-à-vis the elements of S.M.A.R.T. goal-setting strategy. Evaluate how well Amy had implemented these principles of this strategy. Indicate the good points and the points for improvement for each element. You may use the guide questions above as a point of reference in your evaluation when setting your goals.

- Specific?

_____
_____
_____
_____

- Measurable?

_____
_____
_____
_____

- Achievable?

_____
_____
_____
_____

- Realistic?

_____
_____
_____
_____

- Time-Bound?

_____
_____

Chapter 8

Practice Mindfulness

"Remember then: there is only one important time—now! It is the most important time because it is the only time when we have any power."

—Leo Tolstoy

What is Mindfulness?

When your mind is fully focused on what is currently happening to you, on what you are doing, and on the environment where you live in, you are experiencing the phenomenon called mindfulness.

It might seem like something that anyone can do naturally. After all, everyone possesses the potential to achieve this quality through practice.

However, the human mind is prone to wandering. At that point, you will lose touch with what your body is feeling and going through. If this goes on further, obsessive and intrusive thoughts will begin invading your mind, filling it with negative thoughts and worries about the future. In time, this can lead to full, blown anxiety.

Fortunately, no matter how far your mind has gone, mindfulness can bring you back to the present, where you can be, once again, completely aware of your actions and feelings.

Why You Need to Practice Mindfulness

Practicing mindfulness allows you to have better access to its benefits. According to experts, mindfulness can:

- Reduce your level of stress;
- Enable you to gain insight about your inner self;
- Improve your self-awareness, particularly about your thoughts;
- Enhance your physical and mental performance;
- Make you feel happier;
- Increase your level of patience;
- Make you more accepting of the changes in your life; and

- Lower down your feelings of frustration and disappointment.

Mindfulness also fosters your ability to see things from the perspective of others. Through this, you may be able to relieve yourself of your negative thoughts and worries about how others think or feel about you.

For example, your friend snapped at you when you had asked her about her day. At first, you might worry about whether or not you have done something to upset her.

However, if you could set aside this automatic response for even a moment, then you might be able to recall that she mentioned something about having a hard time finishing up a paper. You could then surmise that her foul mood may have resulted from being stressed out by her deadline.

This alternative explanation of your friend's behavior may help alleviate your earlier worries about your actions towards her. You would also feel less bad about being unintentionally snapped at by your friend.

Effective Techniques for Practicing Mindfulness

Even though mindfulness is an innate human ability, you can still improve your access to it by applying various techniques, such as:

- Mindful Meditation

    This technique works best if you would do it in a quiet spot that is free from clutter. It should be well ventilated and well lighted, ideally by natural light.

    Once you have found the perfect spot for this, you must follow these steps to perform mindful meditation properly:

    o Take a seat.

        It can be a chair, a bench, or a floor cushion, as long as it is stable and comfortable.

    o Adjust the position of your legs.

        If you are sitting on a chair or a bench, it is best to keep both feet on the ground. If you are sitting down on the floor, then you should cross both your legs in front of you.

- Adopt a straight posture for your upper body.

    Do not overdo it by straining your spine out of its natural curvature. The angle of your head and shoulders must feel comfortable to prevent their positions from being a source of distraction for you later on.

- Place your upper arms in a parallel position to your upper body.

- Gently place your hands on top of your legs.

    Maintain the positioning of your upper arms from the previous step. This will keep you from either slouching forward or leaning too far back.

- Slowly drop your gaze along with your chin.

    You may also lower your upper lid, or even close them if it would make you feel more comfortable. Take note, however, that this is not necessary for mindful meditation.

- Relax, and be there at the moment.

  Observe if you would feel any unusual sensations in your body.

- Feel and follow your breathing.

  Take note of the air flowing in through your nose or mouth. Observe how your chest or stomach rise and fall with each breath you take.

- When other thoughts enter your mind, do not block them.

  Instead, just gently realign your focus on your breathing once you have noticed that you have drifted away.

- If you need to move your body, take a quick pause before acting upon it.

  There are times when you have to move a body part to feel more comfortable. Sometimes, you would also feel an itch that you just have to scratch. You are allowed to move your body as long as the movement is deliberate and intentional on your part. The pause that you will take before each movement would enable you to make this transition a success.

- When you feel relaxed yet focused, you may lift your gaze and chin once more.

If you had closed your eyes, then you may now open them. Once you do, take note of how your body feels during that moment. Notice the first thoughts and emotions that will rise to the surface as well.

Based on what you have noted, decide on how you should proceed with the rest of your day.

In case you want to incorporate music into your mindful meditation session, then you can try using the iOS and Android app called "Relax Melodies." Unlike most other meditation apps that include guided meditation tracks, this one only contains background music that you can use while meditating. Therefore, this is an excellent option for those who already have experience in mindful meditation but want to enhance their experience further. Since this app is for free, feel free to try it and see if it would be of any use to you.

- Mindful Observation

Through this exercise, you will be able to gain a better and deeper appreciation of even the simplest elements in your current environment. Thus, you will feel a connection with the natural beauty of the things around you—something that would not have been possible because you always seem to be in a rush to go somewhere else.

To do this, you must:

- Choose a natural object that can be found within your field of sight.

    This can be a plant, the clouds in the sky, or even an insect.

- Focus and observe it for a minute or two.

    Do not engage in anything else while you are doing this. Try to relax your body and mind as you do so.

- Look at the object with awe and wonderment, as if this is the first time that you see it.

- Explore with your eyes the form of the object.

Let your attention be consumed by its mere presence.

- o Allow yourself to connect with the object in terms of its role in the natural world, and based on the general vibes that you are getting from it.

- Mindful Listening

This technique involves the presence of two elements: attention and intention. If you can stay in the present, and remain open and unbiased no matter what you hear, then you have the element of focus.

On the other hand, the element of intention is present when you possess a genuine interest in what the other person is saying.

Mindful listening, however, is not simply listening well to others. It also pertains to an individual's ability to listen well to himself/herself. If you are not aware of your personal beliefs, needs, aspirations, and fears, then you will not have much capacity to listen to somebody else's.

To help you apply this technique, here are some essential tips about mindful listening:

- Check inward first.

    If you are feeling something off or unpleasant, then you have to address that first before engaging with others.

- Get a feel of your own presence.

    Let the other person feel your interest and feelings of empathy, too.

- Take note in the silence of any reactions you might have.

    Quickly note your reactions as they arise, and then return your attention to the speaker.

- Make the other person feel heard.

    You may do this by reflecting upon the speaker's words and saying back a summary of his/her main points.

- Keep things going by using open-ended questions.

You may ask questions to clarify points that you do not understand and to probe for more information.

- Mindful Breathing

You may practice this in whatever position is most comfortable for you. Keeping your eyes open or closed also depends on which one would make you concentrate more.

As a guide, here is a short step-by-step process on how to do mindful breathing:

- o Assume a comfortable position that will relax your body.
- o Pay attention to the shape of your body and the sensations that you can feel across different body parts.
- o Switch your focus to your breathing.
- o Feel the natural flow of air in and out of your body.
- o Take note of the sensations in between each breath.

- If your mind starts drifting off to other topics while doing this exercise, acknowledge first that you are straying off from the path by whispering under your breath "wondering" or "thinking." Then, gently realign your focus back to your breathing.

- After around 5 minutes, switch your attention back to the rest of your body.

- Feel how more relaxed you are now.

- Proceed with the rest of your day more mindfully.

- Mindful Walking

This technique is particularly useful because you will walk at some point during the day. You can better utilize that time spent walking by engaging your body and mind with a mindful and meditative exercise.

To guide you through this here is one form of mindful walking that you can do even while walking down a street:

- Assume a straight posture.

- Curl in the thumb of your left hand, and then close the rest of your fingers over it.

- Place your left hand in the spot above your belly button.

- Place your right hand over your left hand, resting the right thumb in the space between the left thumb and the left index finger.

- Slightly drop your gaze.

- Take your first step using your left foot.

- Take another step using your right foot.

- Follow a steady, mindful pace.

- If your mind wanders off, bring it back by focusing again on the sensations of your feet as they touch the ground.

- Guided Meditation

If you do not know where and how to start meditating properly, you may consider trying guided meditations. Through this, you will be able to practice conjuring up mental imageries as you meditate or incorporate different breathing exercises into your routine. Others also teach you how to create personal mantras that you can use for meditation.

There are various sources of guided meditations, including:

- Apps

    Go through the app store on your phone or tablet to find one that would suit your needs. Take note, however, that the popularity of the app does not indicate its quality. Read through the description, and if possible, reviews from actual users to get a better sense of what you may expect from the app.

    Here are some of the suggested apps geared for beginners:

    a. "Mindfulness Training"

        You can get the first two lessons for free in the iOS app store. From these two lessons, you will be able to get 6 sample guided meditations that you can try out for yourself.

b. "Headspace"

This app may be downloaded for both iOS and Android devices. Its main purpose is to be your personal trainer when it comes to your daily meditation practice. You can get this out for free for the first ten days. After that, you will have the option to proceed by subscribing to it for a month, a year, or even a lifetime.

c. "Simply Being"

Through this app, you may be able to customize your meditation experience. You can set your preferred duration for each session, as well as the sounds that you can hear to make the session more immersive. You may choose from nature sounds, guiding voices, music, or a combination of any of these three. This is available on the iOS and Android platforms for $1.99.

- Podcasts

    There are various podcasts available nowadays on the topic of meditation, as well as quick guided meditation practices that you can use to learn the ropes in your own time. Here a few suggested podcasts you can try out based on their popularity. A simple search of these on Google would direct you to where you can listen to these podcasts.

    a. The daily meditation podcast with Mary Meckley

    b. 10% happier with Dan Harris

    c. Tara Brach

    d. The meditation Oasis

    e. Meditation Minis

- Reflect on Your Thoughts

The objective of this mindfulness exercise is to establish a deeper connection with your thoughts. Here are some tips that you can do to practice this:

- You can start this by asking yourself first about the things that you are grateful for.

- To prevent the logical part of your brain from answering, experts suggest referring to yourself in the second person.

  As such, the correct form of a possible starting question is, "What are you feeling most grateful for right now?"

- Thoughts related to this question would surely come to the forefront of your mind.

- Stay connected to the natural flow of your thoughts.

  Avoid trying to direct it in a different direction.

- Form a deep connection with your thoughts as you continue paying your complete attention to them.

To keep yourself from being immersed in this activity for too long, you may use an app, such as the "Insight Timer," to preset a duration for each session. The benefit of using apps like this is that its method of notifying you is significantly less jarring than the alarm timer on your phone. As a result, you will be able to retain the mindful state that you have entered, even after the session has ended.

- Self-Compassion Break

    This technique serves as a personal reminder to apply mindfulness, kindness, and common humanity—the three core components of self-compassion—whenever you are facing difficulties in your life.

    For this method to be effective, you have to make use of the soothing properties of human touch. You must also find a way to communicate with yourself effectively. It will only distract you if you cannot agree with yourself about the meaning of your words.

    Here is a step-by-step process on how to conduct a self-compassion break. Ideally, you should be doing this with your eyes closed to focus more on your inner self.

    o Think of a personal life situation that is making you feel stressed out.

This may be a health issue, problems with your partner or family member, financial difficulties, or work struggles.

- Select a specific problem within that aspect.

  It should not be that big of a problem. You have just started doing this, so it is best to stick to the mild to moderate range for now.

- Visualize your chosen situation.

  Picture in your mind the setting of the situation. If there is dialogue involved, identify the speakers and who is saying what to whom. Go into the details of what is happening and what might happen.

- Take note of the sensations in your body.

  Are you feeling any sort of discomfort while you are visualizing the situation in your mind? If you do not, then you should go back to step 2 and choose a slightly more stressful problem.

- When you feel discomfort in your body, recognize it for what it is.

You may try saying the following statements, whichever sounds right to you. By doing this, you are exhibiting mindfulness.

    a. "This is a moment of suffering."

    b. "This moment is painful for me."

    c. "This is so stressful."

- To channel your common humanity, acknowledge that struggle is part of the normal human experience.

    You may do so by saying out loud any of these statements:

        a. "Suffering is a part of being human."

        b. "I am not alone. Everyone suffers at some point in their lives."

        c. "Other people feel this kind of pain, too when they are struggling."

- Offer yourself a gesture that would soothe yourself, along with a message of kindness to yourself.

    This may be expressed through the following sample statements:

a. "May I accept myself as I am."

b. "May I be kind to myself."

c. "May I be patient. May I be strong."

d. "May I provide for myself whatever I need."

If you cannot think of the right words to say to yourself, then imagine offering support to a family member or a close friend who is suffering from a similar problem as you. What are the words that you will choose then? How can you deliver your message of kindness to those you care about?

Think about this, and see if you can offer the same kind of treatment and support to yourself.

- Body Scan

  Through similar principles of meditation, this technique can enable you to establish a deep connection with your body. As the name implies, it involves a conscious scanning of your body, from the top of your head to the tip of your toes.

  During the process, you will become hyper-aware of any unusual sensations, discomfort, and pains within your body. These are crucial pieces of information because, depending on their location, these may be indicators of an anxious mind and a worn-out body.

To apply this technique, allocate at least 30 minutes for this activity. It is also best to lie down on a mat or a bed, but you may also do this in a sitting position. Choose whichever position would allow you to stay awake and alert throughout the following activity.

- Close your eyes.

    This will help you keep your focus on what matters. If you are not comfortable with this, you may just half-close your eyes.

- Take note of your breathing and your point of contact with the surface you are lying on or sitting on.

    Take as much time as you need to examine the movement and specified areas of your body.

- Once you are ready, take a deep breath before moving on to the examination of another body part.

You can either follow a system wherein you examine everything from your head down to your toes, or you may choose which areas to observe randomly.

- Take note of any sensation you are currently feeling in the body part you are examining.

These sensations include, but are not limited to, tightness, tingling, high or low temperature, pressure, or buzzing. If you cannot feel anything, then that is perfectly fine. Take note of that too.

Your objective for this step is to simply notice your current feelings and sensations. Do not judge anything yet at this point.

- After you have explored the sensations from different parts of your body, expand the scope of your attention to your whole body.

Spend a few minutes just breathing in and out freely as you get an overall feel of your bodily sensations.

- You may now proceed with the rest of your day.

Make your movements more deliberate than usual to retain your current mental state for a longer period.

Case Study

Another strategy that Amy had taken up was practicing mindfulness. Since she was a beginner, she selected guided meditations as her preferred method. She downloaded an app on her phone and set a schedule for her session.

Though she found it hard to achieve a mindful state during her first try, she did notice that she felt more relaxed and calmer after the activity. Because of this, she decided to include this in her weekly to-do list.

Practice Test

Download at least one of the suggested apps for guided meditation given earlier in this chapter. Just like Amy, try out a session, and then answer the following questions based on your experience:

- How do you feel after doing this activity?
- Do you think you have met your goal for this activity? Why or why not?

- Would you try doing this again until it becomes one of your habits? Why or why not?

Chapter 9

Be Happy

If we would just slow down, happiness would catch up to us.

— Richard Carlson

As confirmed by multiple studies, happiness is crucial to one's overall mental health. Happy people tend to have better relationships with the people around them. They find it easier to pursue their true passions in life, and therefore find success in what they have chosen to do. Their happiness also protects them from harmful elements that could lower down the quality of their life, such as overthinking and anxiety.

Attaining happiness in your life is not an easy feat to achieve. Some people assume that there are special techniques that will make them happy overnight. However, that is what makes happiness elusive to them.

Rather than a destination that you need to go to, happiness is found in the journey itself. It is a way of life that makes you feel fulfilled and contented. No matter what your status in life is, you can find happiness with the people around you and in the things that you do.

Live Your Best Life: There Is Only One to Live

You need to make the most out of the life you currently have by finding happiness, purpose, and satisfaction in your life.

A lot of people tend to forget that they have a choice on how to live their lives. They let themselves be stuck in their miserable situations, complaining and whining about how unfair everything is around them.

It is natural for humans to dream for the best possible future for them. However, this can only go so far if that is the only thing that you will do. You have to take action and live your life in the best possible way. This goes beyond simple wishful thinking. It involves finding your true purpose in life and pursuing your passions.

Living up to your full potential is only one way to go about this, though. You can also aim to live a well-balanced life. By figuring out the right balance in the key areas of your life, you would be able to go after the things that will make you happy and fulfilled.

To live your best life, you must commit to creating this kind of life for yourself. You have to commit to facing the challenges of personal growth and development. Only then can you have the strength, courage, and determination to live your best life.

Steps You Can Take to Be Happy

You are in charge of finding your happiness. To guide you through this, here are some actionable steps that you can take right now:

- Add more foods that are rich in tyrosine into your diet.

  Tyrosine is an amino acid that increases the production of dopamine—or also known as the feel-good hormone—in your brain. Excellent sources of tyrosine include almonds, avocados, bananas, and eggs.

- Practice relaxation exercises regularly.

  You may go for a nice massage or a long walk in the park. Meditation has also been proven to be an effective way of calming both the body and the mind.

- Get enough high-quality sleep.

This means that upon waking up, you feel well-rested and more energized. To achieve this, some people set a regular sleeping schedule that enables the REM cycle to complete its course. Others design a sleeping ritual that would put the body and mind into the optimal sleeping condition.

- Make your fitness a priority.

    Exercising regularly increases the dopamine levels in your brain. You do not have to get a gym subscription for this to be effective. You can go for simple activities such as power walking, running, lifting weights, or swimming.

- Practice mindfulness.

    Pay complete attention to everything you do. Avoid giving in to distractions and immerse yourself with the moment. You can practice this by adopting any of your preferred mindfulness techniques elucidated in the previous chapter.

- Be grateful

    Keep track of the things that you feel thankful for.

This may be the people you cherish in your life, or the places you frequent to, or the work projects that you are currently enjoying. For better results, record them in a journal. By doing so, you will be able to refer to them as well whenever you need a little boost.

- Stop comparing yourself with others.

  There is no point comparing yourself with other people because everyone is likely at different phases in their lives. Comparing yourself against someone who is more established in life would only make you miserable.

- Work for meaningful goals, not money.

  You will be more fulfilled if your work is aligned with your purpose in life. No matter how demanding it is, or how little you get paid for doing it, pursuing your vocation would significantly increase your chances of finding happiness.

- Spend more time with positive people.

  One of the basic human needs is socializing. However, it is not just simply the amount of time you spend but also the quality of the time you spend with them. This means that you have to engage in constructive and uplifting activities to generate happiness within you.

The personalities and interests of the people you associate with also factors into your happiness. Ideally, you should select positive-thinking individuals who share similar values as you do.

- Keep good memories, and let go of the bad ones.

    Your memories are your constant companions. Therefore, they can influence your mood and outlook in life in significant ways. Cherish the good memories you have so that you will have a source of inspiration and motivation, especially in times of need.

    Letting go of the negative ones would free you from the burden of having to carry them with you every day. It would also give you more opportunities to appreciate your life in general.

Case Study

Though Amy had begun keeping a list of her blessings, she felt like she was not taking a proactive approach to her happiness. At this point, she was only waiting until something good had happened to her.

To live her best life, Amy started forming a happiness plan. Using her knowledge about effective task management and goal setting, she identified the various ways she can seek out happiness in everything she did.

Feeling more satisfied with this approach, Amy set out to implement her plan to be happier not just at work but in all important areas of her life.

Practice Test

Create your happiness plan using the following table format. You may choose only one area in your life to focus on this exercise. However, feel free to explore all the ways you can think of, as long as you would follow through with the prescribed format.

Area	Goal	Action Plan (To-Do List)
		1.
		2.
		3.

	1.
	2.
	3.
	1.
	2.
	3.

Once you have created your plan, answer the following questions:

- Why did you choose these particular areas (s) in your life to be included in the happiness plan?

- Evaluate your happiness goal vis-à-vis the S.M.A.R.T. goal criteria:

    o Specific?
    _____
    _____
    _____

    o Measureable?
    _____

_____
_____

- Achievable?

_____
_____
_____

- Realistic?

_____
_____
_____

- Time-Bound?

_____
_____
_____

- Based on how well you have made your goals, how do you feel about the happiness action plan that you have made?

Chapter 10

Reach Out to Someone

People suffering from anxiety find it hard to seek out for help due to various reasons. Their tendency to overthink keeps them from acting upon their need for help. They also become more bound to the stigmas associated with mental health issues.

Moreover, the negative thoughts may prevent them from voicing out their concerns out of fear and paranoia, both of which are typically rooted in stigmas and the kind of mental conditioning they have had in their life. This would then translate to worries about being rejected by the people around them and being isolated from those they care about.

In case you are one of these people, know that there are plenty of ways to ask for help. The most accessible one is through the support of your family and friends. However, if you are not comfortable with that, then affordable—sometimes free—therapies conducted with the guidance of a mental health expert are also available nowadays. There are even methods now that allow people to speak out anonymously.

To help you better identify the many ways you can reach out to someone about your mental health issues, the following sections cover the important things you need to keep in mind, especially during challenging times.

Don't be Afraid to Ask for Help

Getting over your fear and worries about reaching out to others is a crucial step in stopping yourself from engaging in overthinking and feeling anxious. As mentioned earlier, the most accessible group of people that you can connect with are those who love you and care about your wellbeing.

To guide you through this, here are the steps you need to take to start effectively communicating with them about this sensitive topic.

- Identify the members of your family and friends that you can trust.

- Schedule a private chat with them on a date and time that is convenient for both of you.

- Open up an honest conversation by admitting that you need help in overcoming your tendency to overthink, your feelings of anxiety, your negative thoughts, and your worries.

- Describe in detail how these mental issues are affecting you in terms of the important aspects of your life, such as your relationships, vocation, and health.

- Be specific about what you need from them so that they can offer you better support.

- Share your safety plan with them so that they will know what to do in case you suffer from panic attacks or any other severe side-effects.

- Promise to keep them up to date about your goal to overcome these issues.

If you are not ready to lay all of these out to the people who know you personally, then you may try joining support groups that are composed of other people who are suffering from similar issues.

In these groups, confidentiality is of the utmost importance to make every member feel safe whenever they open up about their personal experiences. It takes a different kind of courage to admit to strangers the troubles and mistakes in your life. However, the following benefits of doing so typically outweigh these reservations.

- You will likely feel less judged and more understood.

- You are actively encouraged to be open and honest about your thoughts and feelings, no matter how dark and depressing they are.

- The other members are going to share practical tips that have worked for them, and thus may work for you.

- You will get access to relevant resources, such as self-help books and therapists, that can help you resolve your issues.

- After some time, you might feel less lonely and isolated.

Take note that it may take you a while before you can find a support group that will match your needs and preferences. Fortunately, there are plenty of ways to find one that might be compatible with you. You may search online for existing support groups near you, or you may try checking local mental health centers for recommendations. If you are comfortable asking your trusted family members and friends about this, then you may also ask for their advice.

Talk to a Physician If Everything Else Fails

If talking to your loved ones and support groups do not cause any significant improvements, then seriously consider seeking the help of mental health professional.

There are various types of physicians and therapists that you can look for. Each one has its own specialty, but most people who suffer from overthinking and anxiety are advised to get help from those with a background in cognitive-behavioral therapy. This branch of psychology is considered by many as one of the more effective approaches to mental health issues.

Much like support groups, it can be challenging to find a therapist that is compatible with you. You can start finding one through the same methods you have employed in searching for support groups.

Some therapists offer phone consultations so that you can try their services out first before committing to a series of therapy sessions. In case you are not comfortable speaking on the phone with a relative stranger, then an email consultation with a therapist is also pretty common nowadays.

Case Study

Amy has still not resolved her issues with her colleagues at this point. Since her first plan did not work as intended, she sought the help of her best friend, Danny.

After confiding in him about her experiences at work, Amy was surprised to find out that Danny had faced similar challenges when he was just starting at the architectural firm he is working at.

Although different settings, Danny shared with Amy some tips on how he had handled the situation back then. He had also reminded her that she did not have to please everybody and that their opinions would only matter if she would let them get to her.

Feeling well supported and understood, Amy felt more confident that she could get through this issue as well as Danny had done. If not, she knew that he would always have her back.

Practice Test

Answer the following questions about this interaction between Amy and Danny:

- Was Amy right about confiding her work problems to her best friend, Danny? Why or why not?

- Are Danny's pieces of advice actionable for Amy? How do you think Amy would translate Danny's advice into her goals and to-do list?

- Based on all that you have learned so far from this book, what advice would you give to Amy, aside from the ones given already by Danny?

Conclusion

"No one saves us but ourselves. No one can, and no one may. We ourselves must walk the path."

– Buddha

I'd like to thank you and congratulate you for transiting my lines from start to finish.

I hope this book was able to help you understand the causes and effects of overthinking, anxiety, negative thoughts, and worrying in different aspects of your life. I also hope that you were able to find a useful technique that can help you overcome them once and for all.

At this point, you are now better equipped to take control of your thoughts and emotions. In this book, you have learned how to:

- Accept the past, live in the present, and plan better for the future;
- Follow through on your tasks and plans up to completion;

- Optimize your home, relationships, work-life, digital space, and health;

- Set significant and achievable goals in your life; and

- Be more open and honest about your thoughts and feeling to the people who are willing to help you through this.

The next step is to maintain your personal journal as you apply your preferred techniques that have been discussed in the previous chapters of this book. You are free to experiment with which of these strategies would work best with your needs and current situation.

Finally, I want you to take responsibility for your personal wellbeing. Take charge of finding a way to stop overthinking and overcome your anxieties, negative thoughts, and worries by following through with any applicable techniques discussed in the previous chapters. Since you know yourself best—your strengths, limitations, and fears—you know better than anyone which techniques would get you closer to a future that is free from paralyzing thoughts and negative vibes.

Remember, "Knowing is not enough; we must apply. Willing is not enough; we must do", a quote by Goethe.

I wish you the very best!

Printed in Great Britain
by Amazon